GROWTH MINDSET

HOW TO DEVELOP (AND USE) THE GROWTH MINDSET TO UNLEASH YOUR FULL POTENTIAL

DANNY DOUCETTE

Copyright © 2020 by Danny Doucette

All rights reserved.

No part of this publication may be reproduced, distributed, or transmitted in any form or by any means, including photocopying, recording, or other electronic or mechanical methods, without the prior written permission of the publisher, except in the case of brief quotations embodied in critical reviews and certain other noncommercial uses permitted by copyright law.

For permission requests, write to the publisher, addressed "Attention: Permissions Coordinator," at the address below.

ISBN:

CONTENTS

Introduction vii

Section 1: Your Beliefs Matter; Here's Why 1

Chapter 1: A 9/11 First Responders' Example 5

- Limiting Beliefs Lead To A Mediocre Life 12
- Your Thoughts and Words Create Your World 14

Chapter 2: Brandy's Capture Story 17

- A Midnight Trip in Terrorist Territory 18
- A Growth Mindset Can Save Your Life 22
- Fulfilled Potential Is a Result of Positive Beliefs 25
- Internal Changes Precede External Ones 26

Section 2: A Brief Introduction to Mindsets 29

- Understanding Mindsets 30

Chapter 3: The Fixed Mindset 33

Chapter 4: The Growth Mindset 37

- Tom Brady and the Growth Mindset 39

**Section 3: Practical Ways to Develop (and Use)
The Growth Mindset to Unleash Your Full Potential**.... 45

Chapter 5: Self-Insight Is the First Step 49

Chapter 6: Exercise Your Power of Choice 53

Chapter 7: Change Your Perspective Towards Failure 59

Chapter 8: Embrace Lifelong Learning..................................... 63

Conclusion.. 67

INTRODUCTION

Charles R. Swindoll's wise words, *"Life is 10% what happens to you and 90% how you react,"*[1] is my life's mantra. I choose these words as my mantra not because the quote is nice-sounding and catchy, which it is, but because of the infallibility of the statement.

Indeed, *your thoughts, emotions, actions,* and *reactions create your life!*

The life you live, or rather, create for yourself, is less about external circumstances playing out in your life, and more about your inner world. It's about your thoughts, actions, and responses to external conditions.

If your thoughts, actions, and reactions are healthy and positive most of the time, you'll create and live a great life. I said most of the time because let's face it, even the most perfect of us makes mistakes. To err is to be human!

---

[1] Charles R. Swindoll Quotes: https://bit.ly/2W7HWIL

On the other hand, if your thoughts and reactions are negative —as opposed to being thought-out and positive— without a doubt, you'll create a life teeming with insurmountable-seeming odds.

The trick to living a good life, therefore, is to be deliberate with your thoughts and how you approach the circumstances that make up your everyday life. If you live deliberately, mindful of your thoughts, actions, and responses, you can create the life of your dreams.

From personal experience and working with many coaching clients, I've come to realize that to be deliberate and intentional with your life, you need to "get your mind right." That's because when your belief system is right, you're likelier to think healthy thoughts, make the right decisions, and take the right actions.

In other words, to unleash and tap into your full potential, you should work to ensure that your inner compass is pointing in the right direction. When that is the case, no matter how long it takes, because you'll be heading in the right direction, you'll no doubt complete the journey successfully.

Now, I know what you're thinking:

"Danny, that's all great and all, but what do I need to do to ensure my inner compass points in the right direction?

What should I do to ensure that I'm deliberate with my thoughts, actions, and reactions?"

That's a fantastic question. Here's the answer:

To ensure your inner compass is pointing in the right direction, you need to work on your belief system. To make sure your thoughts, emotions, actions, and reactions are positive, you need to become deliberate. You need to adopt a belief system that helps you realize that the only limitations to your potential are those you place on yourself.

A **growth (or positive) mindset** is the universal name given to a belief system driven by positive thoughts, emotions, and actions.

Today, I'd like to speak with you about what you can do to develop and use a growth mindset to unleash and tap into your full potential to create the life you've always desired.

Among tons of other things, from this book, you'll learn:

- What mindset is, why it matters, and the different kinds of mindsets,
- How to develop a growth/positive mindset and apply it to different areas of your life,
- The most bleeding-edge growth mindset tools and strategies you can use to spearhead positive change and growth in your life, and,

So much, much more.

With this book, my purpose is to show you the power of belief. Then, I'll equip you with actionable life-strategies you can use to make the shift to a positive mindset that catapults you towards the life you want.

SECTION 1

YOUR BELIEFS MATTER; HERE'S WHY

What thought's would be going through your mind if you had to run into a collapsed, burning building? How about if you were an Air Force medic, and terrorists kidnapped you in the dead of night. What would you be feeling and thinking? Which ideas would be most poignant in your mind then?

Before becoming a Certified Life and Executive Coach, I was an NYPD police officer. Before that, I was a Commandant (CMSgt) at the USAF First Sergeant Academy. Further back, I was a kid growing up in the unforgiving streets of East Hartford, Connecticut, determined to make it out and in life.

If you're like most people, which you are because research shows that on a DNA level, we are 99.9% alike,[2] you're wondering why I'm sharing my "life story" with you.

I didn't mention these things because I want to "awe" you or show you how "amazing" a life I've had (and have right now). I revealed these things because, like you, I have an experience —or two— to share.

As I've made my way through life, I've had the honor of interacting with many truly amazing people. I've also been privileged enough to learn from and be a mentee to some of the most resilient people in these United States of America.

---

[2] Genetics vs. Genomics Fact Sheet: https://bit.ly/2W5GaaM

Working in the Air Force, the NYPD, and now as a Leadership consultant has allowed me to meet many people who've taught me life-changing lessons that have stuck with me. A case in point is Ed, a first responder during 9/11, and Brandy, a surgical services medic whose 6th deployment and 3rd outing as a 'medic for hire' was in Mosul, Iraq at the height of the insurgence. Ed and Brandy's stories are the basis of the questioning prompts at the start of this section.

With their permission, I'll relate their experiences and use them to show you the power of having empowering beliefs and a positive mindset. You can read more of their stories from my book: True Stories of Resiliency[3]:

---

[3] True Stories of Resiliency: https://amzn.to/2YEO6l2

CHAPTER 1

A 9/11 FIRST RESPONDERS' EXAMPLE

Shortly after the second plane hit the South Tower, dispatch sent Ed's engine, engine 219, to the Williamsburgh Savings Bank building where there were reports of a building on fire.

After getting there, realizing the call was a false alarm, and reporting the same to dispatch, Ed and his team of firefighters started making their way to the WTC.

Now:

You don't need anyone to tell you what instinct dictates for most of us: *run away from danger, not towards it!* And yet, here was Ed and his crew, running towards the scene of a terror attack and a collapsing building. Was it training, or was it something more?

Yes, and without a doubt, the training FDNY officers receive, and the sense of duty Ed and his crew must have felt at that defining moment, was a determinant factor.

However, beyond that, I believe there was something more, something we can all learn from and emulate in our daily lives. I genuinely believe that this 'something more' is *the courage to face adversity with an unwavering commitment to triumph! A positive attitude towards life!*

Ed's story gets more interesting.

As Ed and his team were making their way to WTC, they had to take the Brooklyn-Battery Tunnel. When they got about 50 feet away from the tunnel's exit, it went dark, and traffic instantly crawled to a standstill. Can you guess what Ed and his team did? You guessed it:

Despite being unsure of what awaited them on the other end, or if terrorists had bombed the tunnel, Ed and his crew decided to pick up their gear and walk the rest of the way.

I won't retell the whole story here; you can read about it in my other book:

<u>True Stories of Resiliency</u>[4]

---

[4] True Stories of Resiliency: https://amzn.to/2YEO6l2

I would, however, like you to give something some thoughtfulness:

Besides training, what would motivate and drive Ed and the crew of fire engine 219 to embrace the unknown so willingly?

Moreover, as Ed narrates, when they were walking into the now-darkened Hugh L. Carey Tunnel, it was bright and sunny on their end. However, when they came out the other end, it looked as if they'd walked into a snowstorm. Dust from the collapse of the first building had made visibility a challenge, and the wails from people all around made deciding who to help first a painful decision.

Nonetheless, Ed and his fellow firefighters pressed on. They made choices that put them directly in the line of fire should the second tower collapse, which it did, with them in the vicinity.

Again, I won't relate the entire story here. Read it from my other book True Stories of Resiliency. I would, nonetheless, like you to think about this.

If you were in Ed's shoes, and the shoes of the other firefighters and first responders involved in the post 9/11 life-saving mission, what would have been going through your mind?

Would you have believed you could rise to the occasion and apply what you knew to save as many people as you could, be as helpful, and survive the ordeal with your spirit intact?

Would the possibility of the second tower collapsing on you have riddled you with fear-driven immobility? What about thoughts? Which ones would have been apparent in your mind as you heard the sound of the second tower beginning to collapse?

Would you have thought, *"This is it: the moment I meet my maker!"* Would you have thought, *head in the game! Remember your training and rely on it!"*

I can't guess what you would be thinking, but I can tell you this:

Years of personal experience as an airman, an NYPD officer, and now as a Life and Executive Coach working with high-achievers at the C-suite level, have taught me that your thoughts (and thought-processes) matter.

What you think matters immensely. It matters so much that in a situation such as the one Ed and his fellow firefights found themselves in, "thoughts" could have been the difference between life and death.

Thoughts, and the belief systems they foster, are why when the second tower started collapsing 100 feet away from where they were strategizing, none of the firefighters in Ed's crew fled. It's why, instead, they had the mindfulness to put on their facepieces as fast as they could, take a knee, and wait for the worst to pass so that they could resume their task of saving lives.

Thoughts and beliefs are why in the aftermath of the collapse, the eerie silence that followed, and the mind-invading sound of PASS devices,[5] none of the firefighters in Ed' company contemplated the thought of fleeing.

Thoughts are why, despite feeling overwhelmed and unsure of what to do first, Ed and his brothers and sisters in blue had the fortitude to do what they know and do best: *put out fires and save lives.*

I know what you're wondering:

"What does 'thoughts,' as opposed to training, have to do with this crew of firefighters responded to the dire emergency accordingly?"

If you're wondering that, you need to understand something. Your thought process is a result of training. Ed and his crew were able to respond as they did because, besides physical training, they had trained their minds to deal with such situations accordingly. This mental

---

[5] PASS Device: https://en.wikipedia.org/wiki/PASS_device

training is why at that moment, panic didn't set in for Ed or any of the other firefighters.

It's why instead, what they felt is a burning desire to be there, somewhere they could do something for their country and the state they had dedicated their lives to serving.

James Allen, a British philosophical writer, and one of the most influential pioneers of the self-help movement, once said:

> *"Man is made or unmade by himself. In the armory of thought, he forges the weapons by which he destroys himself. He also fashions the tools with which he builds for himself heavenly mansions of joy, strength, and peace." "… As a man thinketh, so he is. As he continues to think, so he remains.…"*[6]

Undoubtedly, the thoughts going through the minds of Ed and his crew of brave firefighters contributed to their effectiveness during this pivotal moment in their lives.

There's also no doubt in my mind that the thought-driven beliefs these brave men and women had before 9/11 significantly contributed to their response-ability. I'm sure their response to the demands placed on them

---

[6] Jame Allen Quotes: https://bit.ly/2YG6ABD

during this trying moment resulted from years of mental and physical preparedness.

Likewise, and as James Allen clearly illustrates in the quote above, your life, actions, behaviors, and response are a result of your thoughts and belief systems.

Given this, we can only conclude one thing:

What you believe is of paramount importance: you cannot become what you believe you can't become. You can't be what you cannot envision yourself being.

If you don't believe you're capable of success, you can't become successful. If you don't believe you're capable of earning more, you can't earn more. If you think you can't be happy, you won't be happy.

That's just the way life is: you can only become what you believe you can become; you can only do what you think you're capable of doing.

That's why if you're committed to living a great, worthwhile life experience, you should desirously guard against any thoughts that can segue into the formation of a limiting belief system.

Let me something very few people understand, which is why so many are living mediocre lives[7]:

---

[7] The Observer on Limiting beliefs that kill dreams: https://bit.ly/3cghjGR

LIMITING BELIEFS LEAD TO
A MEDIOCRE LIFE

When your core thoughts and belief system are negative and limiting, the results will be a limited life, a life of unfulfilled potential. That's not what you want. Is it? I believe not otherwise you wouldn't be reading this book!

You want a life of fulfilled potential. You want to live an aspirational life where you excitedly look forward to each day because you're living your purpose. Don't you? Well, to have that life, what you need to do is infuse positivity into your thought process so that you can develop a positive, growth mindset.

Bear with me as I ask you another salient question that'll help you see the importance of your thoughts and the belief systems they form:

Have you ever been in a rock-and-hard-place type of situation? How about a circumstance that felt as if your world was crumbling in on itself?

Like most people, your life probably has several, if not many, instances where you faced a 'defining' situation that felt out of your control.

How did you handle that situation? What was going through your mind then? Were you thinking thoughts of doom or triumph? Was the voice inside your head saying, *"I'll beat this,"* or was it saying, *"This situation will be the death of me?"*

Whatever the case may be:

If you look back and take note of the sentiments you had during challenging moments of your life, you'll realize that 99% of the time, the actions you took aligned with your most poignant thoughts then.

In that moment of crisis, if you thought, *"Why me. Why does my life suck so much? It's like suffering and failure are my destiny?"* your actions and responses are likely to have been reactive and therefore misaligned with your ultimate desire.

On the other hand, consider the changes possible had you thought, *"OK! That just happened! What can I learn from this? What can I do to move on swiftly and better the situation?"* In this case, you'll realize that because of this positive attitude, the resulting action would have been positive and growth-minded too. That, my friend, is the power of thought and beliefs.

What you think and believe about yourself, your life circumstances, and everything else about life matters a great deal. What you think and speak becomes your life. Hafiz, a 13th-century Persian poet, expresses this sentiment better (and more beautifully) by saying these profoundly deep words:

> *"The words you speak become the house you live in."*[8]

For reinforcement purposes, let me repeat it:

YOUR THOUGHTS AND WORDS CREATE YOUR WORLD

The words you speak, especially to yourself, create your world. If your inner thoughts are negative, it'll lead to the formation of negative beliefs.

Negative beliefs limit your potential; they keep your life confined to a circle of mediocrity. When pessimistic ideologies overpower positive ones, the result is a life of unfulfilled potential that's far different from the life of your dreams, the life you know you deserve.

That is why if you're going to fulfill your highest potential, which, because you're reading this book, I believe you do, you have to realize something:

---

[8] 110 Hafez quotes: https://bit.ly/3fu7fvX

Your life up to this point has been a series of decisions (choices), actions, and reactions driven primarily by your core belief system and less by outer circumstances.

You use your thoughts, and the resulting beliefs created by the ideas you think about most of the time, to make decisions in each moment of life. That is why no matter who you are or what situation of life you're dealing with, you need to guard your mind and thoughts as if they're Fort Knox.

Let me expound on the importance of having a growth-oriented belief system by briefly retelling a story in my other book: True Stories of Resiliency:

CHAPTER 2

BRANDY'S CAPTURE STORY

At the start of this section, I asked you a question. I asked, *"Which thoughts, ideas, and feelings would be in your mind if, as an Air Force medic, terrorists intent on beheading you kidnapped you?"*

This prompting question was not the brainchild of my mind's creative faculties. It emanated from lessons learned from something that happened in real life to Brandy.

In this chapter, I want to tell you that story in brief, and relate it to the importance of having a positive belief system and thought process:

In 2011, I was an instructor at the United States First Sergeant Academy, teaching and equipping future First Sergeants with the knowledge they needed to become competent, effective leaders.

Besides the fulfillment that came from teaching future First Sergeants life-saving lessons, the deployment stories shared by the students was one of the highlights of my role. There was always something new to learn from hearing deployment stories of senior non-commissioned officers. This setting was how I met and heard Brandy's story.

As was the case with Ed's story, I won't retell her story in full. You can read all about it in my other book: True Stories of Resiliency.

Instead, I'll relate just enough to show you why your beliefs matter so much. I hope that by so doing, I'll motivate you to take greater control of your thought processes using the strategies I'll share with you later in the book:

A MIDNIGHT TRIP IN TERRORIST TERRITORY

Brandy's 6th deployment and 3rd outing as a Surgical Services Medic was near Mosul, Iraq, at the height of the terrorist insurgence. During this period, extremists trying to 'get in good with Al-Qaeda' were very fond of beheading westerners on camera.

As a way to minimize risk to personnel, most United States *Marine* Corps *battalions* opted to travel at night or in the wee hours of the morning. The battalion Brandy served in as part of the Forward Surgical Team (FST) also followed this protocol. On one occasion, Brandy's battalion had to make a long, midnight trip through Mosul.

During the journey, the convoy unexpectedly came to a grinding halt. As the vehicles radioed back and forth, Brandy learned that a truck had broken an axle, with the mechanic injuring his shoulder as he tried to fix the automobile.

Immediately after *"MEDIC"* rang through the air, Brandy immediately jumped from the truck and went for her medical bag. The night, as she tells it, was eerie, quiet, and dark, *"as if something sinister had stolen the night."*

Let me take a short pause here and tell you something I've learned about Brandy: she loves embracing the unknown. As she later expressed to the class, one of her goals in life is to *maintain a calm, smooth transitional demeanor during extraordinary events!*

I don't know about you, but considering that life is a series of unknowns, *"the goal to remain calm and controlled during life's extraordinary moments"* seems a worthwhile mission.

Her plan to achieve this goal is simple: purposely seek out chaotic situations and place herself in them so that she can develop the ability to prosper despite them. That was why, while other medics would have shied away from undertaking FST missions in the middle of nowhere, she found the challenge exciting.

It's from this state of mind that Brandy was operating from on that night; she calls it *"the fateful night that changed her, her life, DNA, vision, and future forever."*

To get to the bag, Brandy had to walk around to the back of the truck. As she was making her way, out of the corner of her eye, she noticed some movement, but before she could connect the dots or react fast enough, it was too late: they took her!

Suddenly, a rope wrapped around her throat, constricting it. One man was dragging her, like a sack of potato, away from the convoy as fast as he could, the other man in tow, guarding the "dragger."

Let me pause here, tell you something, and then ask you a question.

NOTE TO MY READER: If you're wondering why I've laced so many prompting questions into this book, it's because I want you to introspect. By introspecting, you'll gain a profound sense of self-awareness. This self-understanding will help you get the most out of reading this book.

I digress. Let's get back to that question I wanted to ask you:

If you were in Brandy's shoes or situation, what would you have done? What would you have been thinking, and what emotions would have been most apparent then?

Would you have thought, *"My life is over!" "How did I let myself get captured?" "Surely, I'm going to die today!"* Would you have thought, *"If I'm smart about this, I can make it out of this alive!" "What can I do to give myself a fighting chance?" "How can I help my team help me?"*

What would you have thought and felt?

You're probably wondering why I asked you this question. After all, you're not military personnel, and therefore, would (perhaps) never find yourself in such a situation.

Well, as you can imagine, in such a moment, your survival over the next couple of minutes would have depended on your thoughts, emotions, and the actions they triggered.

Moreover, while Brandy's "situation" has a life-in-the-military element, the reality is that most of life's defining moments *strike out of nowhere! Out of the ether of darkness!* While your situation may not be terrorist wrapping a rope around your neck, many of life's challenging situations can feel like they're dragging you underwater.

Given this:

Would it be too farfetched to conclude that, at that moment, if you thought, *"they've got me now! My life is over!"* you would have given in to the situation, slackened, and played into your captors' sinister plans?

Would it be ridiculous to conclude that if you were in that moment, thinking, *"Damn! They've captured me! I have to do what I can to get out of this alive! "I have to give my team the best chance of finding me,"* you would not have made it easy for them to take you?

Is it implausible to believe that had you thought the latter type of thoughts, you would have kicked, clawed, and screamed louder than Jill Drake, the loudest screamer on the planet?[9]

A GROWTH MINDSET CAN SAVE YOUR LIFE

Without a doubt, to any growth/positive-minded person who would have found him or herself in that situation, "giving in" would not have been an option. Survival would have been the only option, because of which, the captors would have gotten the fight of their lives. That is the power

---

[9] Guiness World Record For Loudest Screamer: https://bit.ly/2SKza1d

of belief: It can determine and shape your outcome at any given moment. If we're being literal with words here, having a growth-oriented mindset can save your life!

James Allen expressed this sentiment beautifully when he said:

> *"You are today where your thoughts have brought you; you will be tomorrow where your thoughts take you."*[10]

You know that Brandy's mission is to become someone capable of handling life's extraordinary events with a calm demeanor. Given that this is a positive/growth mindset, what do you think she was feeling and thinking?

"Motherfucker! You've got to be kidding me!"

Those were the first thoughts she had. They're also the words that escaped her mouth!

"LEFT, RIGHT, LEFT," she screamed out the directions her captors were taking her in, hoping her teammates would find her. She was also screaming bloody murder, and fighting for her life by clawing at the wall and her captors. She was also aware that somewhere at the back of her mind, she was repeatedly thinking, *"When I get loose, I'm going to kill these motherfuckers."*

---

[10] James Allen quotes: https://bit.ly/3dpf04C

Given this, would it surprise you to learn that Brandy's decisive action, and help from her teammates, helped her survive that situation, bruised, yes, but alive nonetheless? It wouldn't, right?

That, my friend, is the power of belief!

I'm sure that somewhere at the back of her mind, Brandy knew the enormity of what her capture meant. However, because she had a positive mindset towards, open to embracing the unknown and tackling it in calmly, she acted decisively, which saved her life.

At no point did she think, *"Death is upon me."* Instead, she was thinking of what she could do to get loose, not just to save her life, but to kill her captors too. Here's how she puts it:

"The thoughts I was aware of at the time all sounded like, "I'm going to fucking kill you when I get loose..." Over and over, such thoughts kept running through my head looped on rage and adrenaline."

Likewise, no matter which situation (s) of life you're in, to make it out in one piece, you don't need external power; you need inner belief. Yes, as was the case with Brandy, external help can prove invaluable, but above all that, it's not what matters the most. What does is your thoughts and emotional processes, beliefs, and actions/reactions.

You have to realize something most people don't know:

FULFILLED POTENTIAL IS A
RESULT OF POSITIVE BELIEFS

No matter how you define it, to live a life of fulfilled potential, a successful life, you need to align your beliefs with what you want. If you wish to achieve financial success, you have to court and marry thoughts related to economic wealth. If you desire relationship success, your belief system has to align with this aim. Before you can create and live your dream life, your belief system needs to change and align itself with the life you want.

There're no two ways about it!

Tony Robbins, the greater-than-life, Life Coach, expresses this sentiment as follows:

> *"Beliefs have the power to create and the power to destroy. Human beings have the awesome ability to take any experience of their lives and create a meaning that disempowers them or one that can save their lives."[11]*

---

[11] Tony Robbins Quotes: https://bit.ly/2We3LWO

INTERNAL CHANGES
PRECEDE EXTERNAL ONES

No matter what you want, to achieve it, before you make external changes, you need to make internal changes. You need to change your belief system and thought process. You need to ensure your mind is complementary to what you want to achieve.

Dr. David Schwartz, the author of the bestselling book, The Magic of Thinking Big, put it ever so elegantly when he said:

> *Belief, strong belief, triggers the mind to figure out ways and means how to. "... Believe it can be done. When you believe something can be done, really believe, your mind will find the ways to do it. Believing a solution paves the way to the solution."*[12]

That's true!

If you believe you can or cannot do something, you are right! Those are not my words! They're Henry Ford's words. You and I know what Ford achieved in his lifetime: *a legacy that has outlived him!*

---

[12] David J. Schwartz quotes: https://bit.ly/35HG2kZ

You have to realize something about Mr. Ford: he lived a life of fulfilled potential, yes, but despite that, he wasn't that 'well-schooled.'[13] Many thought him an ignorant fool. As it so happens, at one point, Ford sued a Chicago newspaper for calling him an "ignorant pacifist[14]." The jury ruled in his favor when he illustrated that even though he was not a man of education, he had specialized knowledge.

"What does a 1919 lawsuit have to do with me," you ask.

Realize and accept that to unleash your full potential and use it to create the life of your dreams, you need to let go of any limiting beliefs (mindsets) you may have. You need to replace these limiting belief systems with empowering ones that help you create the life you've always wanted. You have to embrace the growth mindset in all areas of your life!

That, my friend, is what I want to talk to you about today: how to develop a positive, growth mindset in different areas of your life.

Before we get started on that in the next section, let's do say this:

---

[13] Ford and specialized knowledge (Excerpt from Think and Grow Rich: https://bit.ly/2WfEBY7

[14] Medium (Issac Qureshi): https://bit.ly/2SK4CfK

I hope that through the discussion we've had in the chapters that make up this section, you've seen why what you believe matters. I hope too that out of this, you're feeling motivated to take charge of your thought process because the thoughts you think about the most develop your beliefs and mindset.

Now that you're feeling pumped about changing your life, let's move on:

SECTION 2

A BRIEF INTRODUCTION TO MINDSETS

We've talked a great deal about the importance of divorcing a negative belief system in favor of a positive, growth-oriented one. From the conversations we've had, you may have developed a clear idea of what a "mindset" is and that generally, we have more than one type of belief system or mindset.

In this section of the book, I want to go over (very briefly) what a mindset is, and then explain the different types of mindsets we can have.

Let's start with defining what a mindset is so that we're on the same page as we move on together:

UNDERSTANDING MINDSETS

Wikipedia has the most generally accepted definition of what a mindset is. It defines it by stating:

> "... a mindset is a set of assumptions, methods, or notations held by one or more people or groups of people. A mindset can also be (an) incident of a person's world view or philosophy of life."[15]

---

[15] Wikipedia's definition of what a mindset is: https://en.wikipedia.org/wiki/Mindset

This definition is as succinct as they come. Your mindset is the set of beliefs, attitudes, and assumptions you have towards different aspects and areas of your life.

We can narrow this definition a bit further by defining a mindset as *"your frame of mind or way of thinking of any given moment or situation."*

Most of what we know about mindsets and the critical role they play in how our lives shape up comes from Carol S. Dweck, a Professor of Psychology and American researcher.

Her research and seminal works in the field of motivation, success, and mindset are some of the most influential in this field.

Dweck defines mindset as follows:

> *"Mindset is a self-perception or "self-theory" that (you) hold about yourself. Believing that you are either "intelligent" or "unintelligent" is a simple example of a mindset."* [16]

This definition plays well into what we've discussed thus far about the power of belief. Believing you can (or not) do

---

[16] Carol Dwecks definition of what mindset is: https://www.edglossary.org/growth-mindset/

something is an example of the mindset you have towards that specific undertaking.

Mindsets form when you steadfastly hold on to a set of recurring thoughts. These thoughts then develop into belief systems, mental attitudes, predispositions, and habits that determine how you interpret and respond to the various situations and circumstances that make up your life.

As we have described, your belief system plays an instrumental role in the decisions and actions you take at any given moment in life. That makes knowing which mindset you have towards different areas of your life paramount.

After all, this collection of beliefs determine your thoughts, feelings, actions, as well as how you make sense of things. Without having a clear idea of the mental models you use to make decisions, we can postulate that you'd make unhealthy choices.

According to Dweck, we have two primary types of mindsets: a *fixed* and *growth mindset*.

Let's discuss these concepts individually very briefly:

CHAPTER 3

THE FIXED MINDSET

In her bestselling book, *Mindset: The New Psychology*[17], Dweck defines the fixed mindset as believing your basic qualities, such as your intelligence, are static. In a fixed mindset, no matter how much time and effort you dedicate to it, you cannot develop your elementary qualities past their innate level.

On why a fixed mindset is not an ideal place from which to operate, Dweck postulates that:

> *"Besides causing you to believe your core characteristics are static, a fixed mindset also does another thing. It causes you to believe that you have no choice but to accept the hand "fate" deals you!"* [18]

---

[17] Mindset: The New Psychology of Success (Carol S. Dweck): https://amzn.to/3duwFbe

[18] Notes from Mindset: The New Psychology of Success: https://bit.ly/2WBoZgo

Out of believing this, you're likely to have negative thoughts and belief systems that chain you to mediocrity, a life of unfulfilled potential.

To illustrate just how damaging a fixed mindset can be, Dweck cites data from some of her students. She states that students with a fixed mindset are likelier to learn at a slower pace. They're also prone to shying away from academic challenges, especially ones likely to highlight what they believe is their "deficient intelligence."

Dweck's research on the fixed mindset compounds the matter further by noting:

When you have a fixed mindset, you're likelier to shun new situations simply because you don't want to fail — because you believe failing means "you're not enough."

Moreover, whenever you face a circumstance or situation that's out of your comfort zone, negative thoughts, such as "I can't __" are likely to run amock in your mind.

One of Dweck's quotes on the fixed mindset notes:

> *"In a fixed mindset, everything is about the outcome. If you fail—or if you're not the best—it's all been wasted."*[19]

---

[19] Carol S. Dweck quotes: https://bit.ly/3fr7KqR

The fixed mindset is everything you should not allow yourself to be. Besides limiting your potential, nothing good can come out of believing that no amount of effort of hard work can lead to self-development. That's why you should replace it with a growth mindset.

Since you now understand the limitations of a fixed mindset, spend some time thinking about the areas of life where you operate from a fixed mindset. The best way to go about this is to ask yourself pertinent questions. For instance:

- What are your beliefs towards core characteristics such as intelligence and creativity? Do you believe you get what you get at birth, and there's nothing you can do to change or improve it?
- Do you believe that no matter how much you learn, you can never change your intelligence level?
- Do you believe that no matter what you do, you cannot change the person you are at your core?

Adopted from Dweck's book, such questions can help you determine the areas of life where you have limiting beliefs. These questions and other similar ones can help you see where the fixed mindset is keeping you from unlocking your full potential. You can also use the Mindset Assessment Test (online)[20] to determine and learn more about your mindset:

---

[20] Mindset Assessment: https://blog.mindsetworks.com/what-s-my-mindset

https://blog.mindsetworks.com/what-s-my-mindset

Once you discover such areas, earnestly embark on the process of swapping these beliefs with the growth mindset.

Let's briefly discuss the growth mindset.

CHAPTER 4

THE GROWTH MINDSET

A growth mindset, according to Dweck's research, *"is the belief that you are more than the "cards" fate dealt you."* When you have a growth mindset, your core character traits are not unchangeable. Instead, you believe that they're just a starting point.

When you have this mindset, you believe that with committed, hard work, you can cultivate any talent, character trait, aptitude, etc.

With a growth-centric mindset, you don't try to convince others of your "intellectual endowment." Instead, you commit time and energy to the actual development of your intellect, skills, and expertise.

A growth mindset develops fro having a positive belief system, positive thoughts, and actions. For instance, when you believe that passionate toiling will lead to mastery in a specific field, this positivity is likely to enhance your persistence.

According to Dweck's research findings:

Out of believing that mastery over any capability can come from diligence, strategic thinking, planning, and decisive action, you're likelier to be more successful. That makes sense because:

Unlike someone who believes that core characters are innate and undevelopable, when your mindset is growth-oriented, your commitment to personal development will be higher. Because of this, once you decide you want to achieve something, you're likely to be like a dog with a bone: unwaveringly committed to the pursuit.

Moreover, when you have a growth mindset, you'll be more open to new opportunities, even ones that call for committing and then learning you're your mistakes.

Moreover, because of believing that success is a result of time and effort, you're likelier to have a penchant for challenges. In situations that call on you to do so, you embrace change, court it even, and work through any obstacles on the path to the success you envision.

Being growth-minded does more than make you positive towards life and open to new opportunities and possibilities. It also makes you grittier, more resilient, and a chronic learner. In essence, it helps you become the proverbial *"boy who wouldn't quit."*

When you believe you can achieve your goals because you are more than willing to exercise dogged determination towards their attainment, you eventually accomplish them.

From this mindset, failure is not a judgment of doom. Instead of focusing on your failures and faults, you focus more on what you can learn from the process. This focus turns failures into invaluable lessons that fuel your success.

Tom Brady is an exceptional example of a growth mindset:

TOM BRADY AND THE GROWTH MINDSET

Today, when American football enthusiasts think of or mention great players, Tom Brady's name usually comes up in the same sentence as Joe Montana.

Without a doubt, notwithstanding the Deflategate scandal[21], Brady is a legendary quarterback in the history

---

[21] The Deflategate Scandal: https://en.wikipedia.org/wiki/Deflategate

of the NFL. Most of his teammates at the New England Patriots, where he spent the first 20 years of his career, consider him a phenomenal decision-maker and thrower. At 42 years of age, he's still one of the best QBs the NFL has ever seen. However:

Did you know that Brady did not have this 'greatness' handed to him on a silver platter? As a matter of fact, in the 2000 NFL draft, he was the 199th draft because he didn't have such commendable measurable. He had slow foot speed, a too-small frame, and an arm strength many scouts considered inadequate to throw a tight spiral.

At the time, many scouts also opined that he had poorly developed improvisation skills, and could thus not prove handy in case a play broke down. Others went as far as to say that his 'OK statistics were because he was playing on a great team.

In retrospect, these criticisms are nothing short of laughable, but they do raise a rather important question:

How did Brady go from a 199th pick to being one of the most recognizable NFL player? The answer is the growth mindset.

There's no doubt that Brady has natural affinities that make him a fantastic QB. For instance, he's tall and can throw a football. These, however, are not what makes him one of the greatest quarterbacks. What separates Brady from the average quarterback is his work ethic, discipline, and mindset. Brady has a growth mindset.

Interviews from his teammates paint Brady as an obsessively hard worker. He's such a dedicated hard worker that Sports Illustrated and other publications have covered his neurotic workout and diet regimen.[22]

According to reports, he's was usually the first to practice facilities, as well as the last to leave. Out of believing he can get better with every game, he was always eager to set incredibly challenging goals for himself. Further, to Brady, failure was not a proclamation of his 'wantedness" but a stepping stone to self-betterment. If that is not an apt description of the growth mindset, what is?

In a post published on The Patriots Way, Kevin Faulk, a former teammate, illustrated why Brady was so exceptional a quarterback by stating:

> *"Back in 2001, when Drew Bledsoe got hurt and Tom took over at quarterback, we knew there was something special about him right away. You could just feel it.*
>
> *We used to run offensive drills where we would run plays against the air. No defense,*

---

[22] Si on Tom Brady's diet and workout routine: https://bit.ly/2WVEakX

just skill guys executing plays. And I can't even tell you how many times we'd run a play and after it was over, Tom would be like, "Kevin! Stop! Let's run that again."

It didn't matter who he was throwing to. If a pass fell incomplete or if something wasn't right, he would stop the show and run the play over and over until we got it right. And if we didn't have enough time, he'd ask us to stay after practice to run it again. Or if there was even a slight miscommunication, he'd take us all into the meeting room after practice and draw the play on the board to see what we got wrong.

Watching him operate this way, we all thought, Damn … this is a guy who was drafted in the sixth round, and he has that kind of confidence and work ethic? That's pretty special.

He wasn't the biggest, strongest or fastest guy. But he always wanted to compete against the biggest, strongest and fastest because he loved the challenge and wanted to make himself better.

So yes, that competitiveness is a huge part of who Tom Brady is.

This is a guy who, when the schedule came during the off-season, would identify the defensive coordinator for each of our opponents and start looking back at film from everywhere that coordinator had coached in the previous five years — just to study tendencies and get a step ahead before the season started. That's how dedicated he is to his craft."[23]

There's no doubt in my mind that despite his poor drafting, having a growth mindset is what helped Brady become one of the greatest quarterbacks the NFL has ever seen.

Like Brady, no matter how "poor a draft you are," by developing a growth mindset, you can change your life in unthinkable ways. That is what I'd like to talk to you about next: *how to develop a growth mindset.*

---

[23] Excerpts from Kevin Faulk (The Patriots Way): https://bit.ly/2Li4EaN

SECTION 3

PRACTICAL WAYS TO DEVELOP (AND USE) THE GROWTH MINDSET TO UNLEASH YOUR FULL POTENTIAL

Dweck's research suggests that mindsets form out of two primary things: beliefs and training. To me, that means no matter how steeped in a fixed mindset you are, you can change it by working on your belief system.

In the chapters that'll make up this section of the guide, we'll discuss practical growth mindset strategies you can use in your daily life. The more you use these strategies in your life, the more you'll reinforce the growth mindset in different areas of your life.

Now, before we start, it's worth mentioning that:

As Dweck's research has shown, we are all a mixture of fixed and growth mindsets: we can't be one or the other. You can have a growth mindset towards your relationship and a fixed mindset towards your career. Being purely growth-minded in all areas of life is a fallacy you're better off not pursuing.

The goal, therefore, is to evolve continuously through experience. As long as you are open to the realization that life is about growth, you should be OK. After all, the growth mindset is exactly that: *believing that no matter what, you can grow and become better!*

Do you believe that no matter how poorly you're doing right now in different areas of life, with hard work and commitment, you can become better? If yes, then that's all you need: a commitment to growth!

The following strategies will help you actualize this commitment and make the growth mindset a mainstay in various areas of your life.

CHAPTER 5

SELF-INSIGHT IS THE FIRST STEP

All forms of growth start with the awareness that something needs to change. After all, you cannot change something you are unaware of or selectively oblivious to at any given point. That is why changing a fixed mindset into a growth mindset starts with introspection and self-insight.

The first step towards introspection and developing deeper self-insight is to spend some time thinking about the areas in your life where you have a fixed mindset.

The goal here is simple:

To tap into, unleash your full potential, and then use it to create the life of your dreams, you need to focus on areas of your life where you're not doing as well as you know you should be doing.

For instance, is your health where you know it ought to be? How about your career? Are you doing as well as you want and know you should be doing? What about your committed relationship or marriage? Are there things about it you wish were better?

The very act of discerning the areas of life where you're not living up to your full potential is enough to show you where you have a fixed mindset.

For the process of self-introspection and insight to be practical, once you become aware of where you're lagging in life, pay attention to the thoughts and beliefs you have towards this area(s). Are they complementary and growth-centric, or are they limiting and steeped in the fixed mindset?

Making this distinction can be a bit challenging, especially if you've trained yourself to see things from a gloom and doom perspective. Given this, when you think about an area of life you'd like to improve, pay attention to what your inner voice says about this change.

Whenever you're about to embark on a new challenge, what does the voice in your mind say? Does it say things like, *"Dude! Be real with yourself! You can't do that!"*

"Stop kidding yourself! You're not naturally fit! Just give up! " You can never achieve that goal no matter how hard you try!" Does it say, "You can do this! All you need is a sound plan!" *"If you are persistent and committed to achieving this goal, you can do it!" "What obstacles will be on the path to this accomplishment? How can I hedge against them?"*

Your inner voice can sabotage and undermine you, or it can motivate and grow you. The trick to developing a growth mindset is to become aware of the nature of this voice, especially in the face of a new undertaking or challenge.

Without self-awareness/insight, recognizing when the voice of the fixed mindset sabotages your chances of growth won't be easy. On the other hand, being mindfully self-aware will make it easier to recognize when your self-talk is being a saboteur.

Mindfulness, formally as mindfulness meditation sessions, and informally as non-judgemental, moment-to-moment awareness, is the best way to cultivate self-awareness.

My suggestion to you is to dedicate 10-15 minutes of your day to the observance of your thoughts. The more you engage in this form of formal mindfulness, the easier it shall become to practice it informally in your daily life.

If you'd like to learn more about how to integrate mindfulness into yor life, read my other book: Life-Changing Mindfulness, 7 Habits and Steps That'll Help You Become More Mindful in 7 Days. [24]

Once you become aware of a fixed, limiting thought and belief pattern that's limiting potential in an essential area of life, the next step is to play into the power of choice:

---

[24] https://www.amazon.com/dp/B08BWLZZ54

CHAPTER 6

EXERCISE YOUR POWER OF CHOICE

've talked a great deal about the power of mindset. I've also gone out of my way to use examples to show you how having the right mindset can make all the difference. All that notwithstanding, you have to realize something:

The mindset you have in any specific area of your life is a result of your core thoughts, the feelings they stir, beliefs they foster, and actions they trigger. This understanding is foundational to changing your mindset because once you understand it, something much more critical will become apparent:

Because you can always choose what you think and feel at any given moment, the *mindset you have towards anything is a choice!* I know what you're thinking:

> *"Danny, that seems like an oversimplification of the change process!"*

You're right. I am simplifying the process, but that's because change itself is not all that complicated; it's simple. Change happens in mere moments. It starts the moment your perception towards something changes. It then carries on to tangible, outer changes.

Changing your mindset, therefore, happens the moment you realize, *"Hey! My mindset towards X or Y is not all that healthy."* Tony Robbins has an impactful quote on how change happens. He states:

> *"...Change happens in a moment! The moment you say 'it's over... Your life changes the moment you make a new, congruent, and committed decision..."*[25]

This fact is why the first step towards changing your mindset is to cultivate deeper self-awareness. Because the moment your ability to notice when your mindset towards an aspect of your life is not complementary to the growth you want to achieve, you can change it.

You always have a choice!

---

[25] Tony Robbins quotes: http://danadinnawi.com/change-happens-moment/

You can choose to believe your inner voice when, ever so loudly, it tells you how you are not talented enough to do that, how you should not attempt that goal because you'll lose, etc.

Likewise, you can choose to question the authenticity of such thoughts. You can choose to accept that in life, very few things are unchangeable stone marbles.

Moreover, once you become aware of the flare-ups of a defeatist, fixed mindset voice, you can choose to question it and seek supportive or challenging evidence. Most often, the views of the fixed mindset buckle the moment you ask directed questions.

My challenge to you is this:

Whenever you become aware of the voice of a fixed mindset, which requires that you be mindful from one moment to the next, take note of it. Then, talk back to it; question what it's saying.

For instance, if the voice says, *"learning a new skill is too challenging. The process is full of setbacks too!"* Acknowledge its opinions, but don't blindly follow its directions. Ask it questions.

For example, *"why is learning a new skill challenging?"* *"Is it because of the setbacks?"* "If so, what can you do to prepare to tackle them?" *"Which challenges and setbacks can you expect, and how can you hedge against them?"*

Do you see what I mean?

By becoming aware of the voice of the fixed mindset, you can choose to view what it says in a different light, a growth mindset light. Since the intention is to use the growth mindset to unleash and then tap into your potential, it's especially critical that you cultivate self-awareness. When you're self-aware, it becomes easier to notice fixed mindset thoughts and to question their authenticity.

Also imperative is that once you notice the voice of the fixed mindset, you talk back to it from a growth mindset perspective. If the fixed mindset voice highlights how you lack the talent to achieve something, remind it how ability is less talent and more practice. If the fixed mindset mentions the possibility of failure in a new endeavor, remind it that success is, above all, a *"result of learning from and persevering through one failure to the next."*

Always remember that you can choose to believe what the voice of the growth mindset says or to question it and talk back to it from a growth mindset perspective. Which of these choices is likelier to lead to actualized potential? You guessed it! Questioning the authenticity of this voice and then countering what it says from a positive frame of mind.

Yes, and without a doubt, developing this ability will take tons of practice, but I believe you're committed to personal growth; otherwise, you wouldn't be reading this book. This commitment to unleashing your full potential is how I know you're ready and willing to commit to the development of this ability.

CHAPTER 7

CHANGE YOUR PERSPECTIVE TOWARDS FAILURE

As a Life and Executive Coach, I've worked with a lot of people at different levels of success and development. From this opportunity to work with various coaching clients, I've learned something influential:

"Fear of, or thoughts of failure" is one of the most significant causes of stymied potential. Coincidentally, thoughts of failure are also one of the catalysts of a fixed mindset. Which is why I now believe that:

To change a fixed mindset into a growth mindset, and to unleash your full potential, you need to change your perspective towards failure. You downright need to embrace failure with both hands.

Can you remember Brandy, the surgical services medic whose growth mindset story you read about in chapter 2? Great! Can you remember the strategy she used to ensure that she could handle life's extraordinary moments with calmness?

That's right! Her goal in life is exposure therapy: to place herself in chaotic situations so that from it, she can enhance her ability to cope well! This strategy can apply to the growth mindset, especially when it comes to failure!

I assume, rightly so, that you want to develop a growth mindset so that you can do precisely that: become better in different, essential areas of your life! Since that is the case, you need to realize and accept that failure is an integral part of the self-development process! Given this, your view towards it needs to change RIGHT NOW!

Developing a growth mindset and unleashing your full potential starts with becoming more self-aware, that's for sure. However, embracing failure is where the *"rubber meets the proverbial road."*

See:

To grow into your full potential in any area of life, you need to embark on new undertakings. What that means is that matter which way you choose to look at it, you will not avoid or escape failure! It an integral, inescapable part of the growth process! Think of it this way:

For a child to go from crawling to walking, what has to happen? That's right, besides using furniture and other household things for support, the child has to fall down a couple of times. Lief is a lot like that!

Most successful people you know failed their way to success. And by success, you have to realize that we mean people who've tapped into and unleashed their full potential, with the outer manifestation of this being tangible success.

The secret to developing a growth mindset, as well as tapping into your full potential, is to stop seeing failure as that. Instead, see it as a means to an end, with the end being the success you desire and deserve in different areas of life.

Always remember what the great Winston Churchill said:

> *"Success is stumbling from failure to failure with no loss of enthusiasm."*[26]

Here's my challenge to you:

---

[26] Winston Churchill quotes: https://www.keepinspiring.me/winston-churchill-quotes/

Whenever the voice of the fixed mindset flares up because you're about to embark on a new challenge, have encountered a setback, or received some not-so-good feedback, challenge it. If it says, "you'll fail," remind it that success is a result of failing from one endeavor to the other without losing motivation. Whenever your inner voice says, "you can't do that because you don't have the ability," remind it that all growth is a result of taking chances.

Again, the more persistently you question the judgments of the fixed mindset, the more pliable it shall be, which is what you want.

CHAPTER 8

EMBRACE LIFELONG LEARNING

Do you know what neuroplasticity is? Have you ever heard of it? Neuroplasticity is your brain's ability to change, adapt, and grow based on various factors such as the demands you place on it.

Dr. Celeste Campbell, a leading neuropsychologist, says:

> *"(Neuroplasticity) refers to the physiological changes that happen to the brain because of our interactions with the environment. From the time the brain begins to develop in utero until the day we die, the connections among the cells in our brains reorganize in response to our changing needs. This dynamic process*

allows us to learn from and adapt to different experiences."[27]

In case you're wondering why this matters to self-growth, changing your mindset, and living up to your fullest potential, here's why:

The fixed mindset is the belief that your abilities are a set of unchangeable stone structures. It's the belief that no matter how big a chisel and mallet you have, and no matter how hard you hit it, you can't change these stone structures. That is not the case.

As neuroplasticity has so clearly proven, by default, your brain is malleable. This malleability means you can learn anything. Even if you're not the best bass guitar player, with time, and because of neuroplasticity, you can learn to play like Paul McCartney. Yes, it may take time and tons of effort, but the fact is that if you're committed enough to anything, by default, you can master it!

To apply neuroplasticity to adopting an empowering one in place of a limiting one, what you have to do is realize that living up to your full potential is a lifelong lesson.

The most standout characteristic of growth-minded people is they are lifelong learners: they understand

---

[27] Celeste Campbell on Neuroplasticity: https://positivepsychology.com/neuroplasticity/

the value of neuroplasticity, *which is why they're always learning!* Here's the thing, my friend:

If you examine the lives of successful people, you'll realize that they dedicate a significant portion of their lives to learning. Research conducted by Thomas C. Corley shows that 85% of successful people read at least two self-development books per month[28]. He notes:

> *"Successful people engage in at least 30 minutes a day of self-improvement reading. ... They read or listen to books, articles, newsletters, etc. They study stuff that helps them do a better job. They go to seminars, speaking engagements, and take courses at night school."*[29]

That is what you need to do to unlock your potential and change your mindset: expose yourself to new ideas by becoming a lifelong learner.

My challenge to you is simple: dedicate a portion of your day, at least 30 minutes, to learning something new. Be especially committed to learning new things that challenge any negative mindsets you may have towards different areas of your life.

---

[28] Tom Corley on habit of the successful: https://bit.ly/2A7qAmv

[29] Tom Corley on habits of successful people (CNBC): https://cnb.cx/2zomaHB

For instance, if you have a negative attitude towards your career growth, commit to learning something new. You can read books that teach you how to do what you do more efficiently. You can take an online course that gives you new skills that improve your career prospects. You get the drift, right?

By embracing lifelong learning, you will always be pushing the needle. You will also feel compelled to seek out novel challenges, which will help you develop a positive mindset and unleash your potential.

Again, moment-to-moment mindfulness is very central to your ability to embrace lifelong learning. That's because by becoming more aware of your thoughts, especially when you're embarking on new challenges, you can notice limiting beliefs. Awareness then helps you begin the process of questioning these limiting beliefs from a positive perspective.

CONCLUSION

Thank you for reading this guide!

From our discussions, I hope you've learned a thing or two about the importance of having a growth mindset.

Besides helping you become more positive in life, having a growth mindset is essential because when you have one, your chances of success are higher. That's because when you believe that you can learn and grow, your likelier to be more resilient and grittier.

To recap, you can develop a growth mindset by:

- Becoming more self-aware: The more self-aware you are, the quicker you'll be able to realize when you're viewing things from a limiting, fixed mindset.
- You always have the power of choice. You, and only you alone, can decide how you view things: you have the power of choice! Always choose to view things from a positive lens.

- Change your perspective towards failure. A fixed mindset is usually a by-product of the fear of failure. Stop seeing failure as a pronunciation of your deficiencies. Instead, view it as a stepping stone to success: embrace this mantra: "I'll fail my way to success."
- Become a lifelong learner. By nature's design, we ought to keep learning from our moment of conception to the moment we pass on from this world. A fixed mindset, the belief that you can learn or change, goes against this tenet, which makes it untenable: let it go! In its place, adopt lifelong learning and dedicate a portion of your day to learning something new that helps propel you into the next phase of personal growth.

If you can follow these four simple steps, I promise, guarantee it even, that gradually, you'll develop a growth mindset in critical areas of life. As you embark on this journey, let me remind you that it's impossible to be growth-minded through and through. That should not be your goal. Your goal, instead, should be to become growth-minded in most areas of life, especially the areas you consider central to your self-actualization.

Thank you again for purchasing, downloading, and reading this book. I trust it was informative and practical.

Lightning Source UK Ltd.
Milton Keynes UK
UKHW012049301122
413111UK00007B/1228